D1558537

Lacrosse

LACROSSE

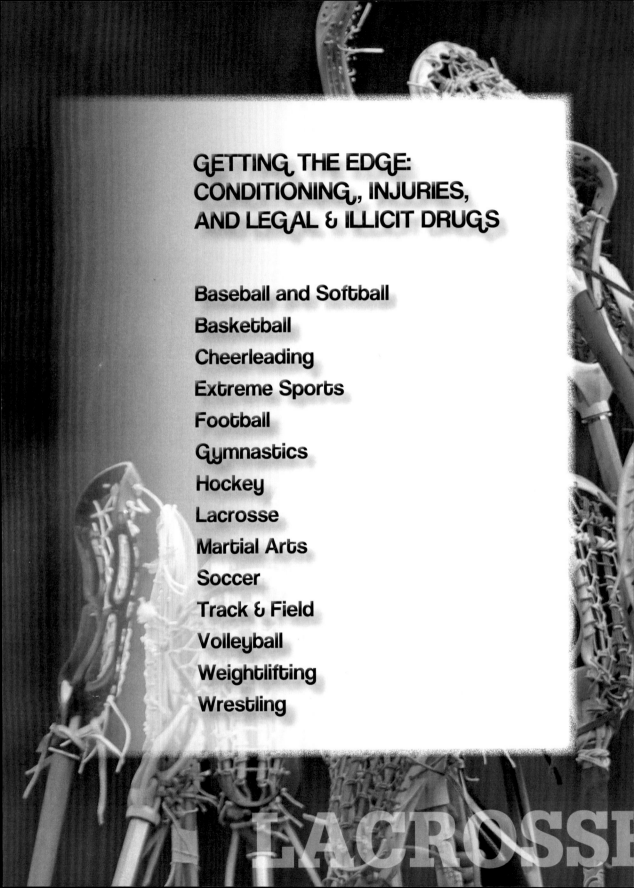

GETTING THE EDGE: CONDITIONING, INJURIES, AND LEGAL & ILLICIT DRUGS

Baseball and Softball

Basketball

Cheerleading

Extreme Sports

Football

Gymnastics

Hockey

Lacrosse

Martial Arts

Soccer

Track & Field

Volleyball

Weightlifting

Wrestling

LACROSSE

Lacrosse

by Gabrielle Vanderhoof

Mason Crest Publishers

MASON CREST PUBLISHERS INC.
370 Reed Road
Broomall, Pennsylvania 19008
(866)MCP-BOOK (toll free)
www.masoncrest.com

First Printing
9 8 7 6 5 4 3 2 1

Library of Congress Cataloging-in-Publication Data

Vanderhoof, Gabrielle.
  Lacrosse / by Gabrielle Vanderhoof.
    p. cm. — (Getting the edge: conditioning, injuries, and legal & illicit drugs)
  Includes bibliographical references and index.
  ISBN 978-1-4222-1737-5   ISBN (series) 978-1-4222-1728-3
  1. Lacrosse—Juvenile literature. 2. Lacrosse—Training—Juvenile litera-
ture. I. Title.
  GV989.14.V36 2011
  796.34'7—dc22
                              2010012754

Produced by Harding House Publishing Service, Inc.
www.hardinghousepages.com
Interior Design by MK Bassett-Harvey.
Cover Design by Torque Advertising + Design.
Printed in the USA by Bang Printing.

Contents

Introduction

Getting the Edge: Conditioning, Injuries, and Legal & Illicit Drugs is a four-teen-volume series written for young people who are interested in learning about various sports and how to participate in them safely. Each volume examines the history of the sport and the rules of play; it also acts as a guide for prevention and treatment of injuries, and includes instruction on stretching, warming up, and strength training, all of which can help play-ers avoid the most common musculoskeletal injuries. Each volume also includes tips on healthy nutrition for athletes, as well as information on the risks of using performance-enhancing drugs or other illegal substances. Getting the Edge offers ways for readers to healthily and legally improve their performance and gain more enjoyment from playing sports. Young athletes will find these volumes informative and helpful in their pursuit of excellence.

Sports medicine professionals assigned to a sport with which they are not familiar can also benefit from this series. For example, a football ath-letic trainer may need to provide medical care for a local gymnastics meet. Although the emergency medical principles and action plan would remain the same, the athletic trainer could provide better care for the gymnasts after reading a simple overview of the principles of gymnastics in Getting the Edge.

Although these books offer an overview, they are not intended to be comprehensive in the recognition and management of sports injuries. They should not replace the professional advice of a trainer, doctor, or nutrition-ist. The text helps the reader appreciate and gain awareness of the sport's history, standard training techniques, common injuries, dietary guidelines,

and the dangers of using drugs to gain an advantage. Reference material and directed readings are provided for those who want to delve further into these subjects.

Written in a direct and easily accessible style, GETTING THE EDGE is an enjoyable series that will help young people learn about sports and sports medicine.

—*Susan Saliba, Ph.D., National Athletic Trainers' Association Education Council*

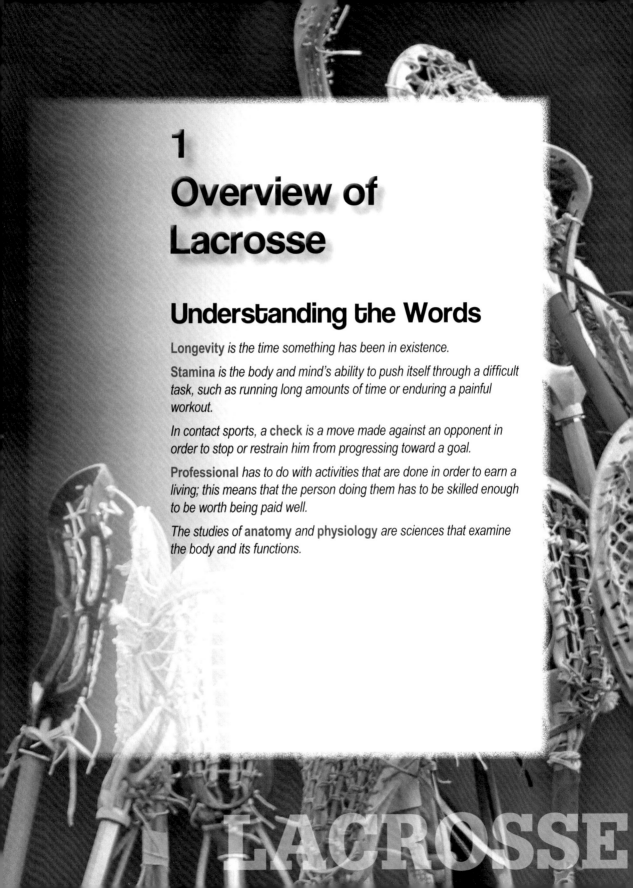

1
Overview of Lacrosse

Understanding the Words

Longevity *is the time something has been in existence.*

Stamina *is the body and mind's ability to push itself through a difficult task, such as running long amounts of time or enduring a painful workout.*

In contact sports, a **check** *is a move made against an opponent in order to stop or restrain him from progressing toward a goal.*

Professional *has to do with activities that are done in order to earn a living; this means that the person doing them has to be skilled enough to be worth being paid well.*

The studies of **anatomy** *and* **physiology** *are sciences that examine the body and its functions.*

LACROSSE

Lacrosse may not be one of the most popular sports in our culture today, like baseball or basketball, for example, but it definitely has the most impressive **longevity**: it is known as "the fastest sport on two feet" and is one of the oldest games known to humanity. Native American tribes started playing the game in what is now the northeastern United States and southeastern Canada long before the first settlers arrived in the New World.

History of Lacrosse

The Algonquians were the first tribe to play lacrosse, but scholars do not agree on which Native American tribe actually invented it; the Hurons and Iroquois may also have been involved with its creation.

The name we use today for the game evolved from the French term *la crosse*, literally meaning "cross." When the settlers arrived in North America, the sticks that Native Americans used in the game reminded them of the cross carried by the French bishops. A Jesuit missionary, Jean de Brebeuf, officially coined the name in 1636.

Intertribal games of lacrosse, known as "baggataways," served two purposes. They were played as a recreational sport, but also as a way to train warriors. The games were played under long, tough, grueling conditions that helped the warriors develop strength, **stamina**, and endurance. In fact, the Cherokees referred to lacrosse as "the little brother of war," because of its military training aspect.

The first recorded game between Native Americans and white French settlers was in 1790. We can assume the settlers suffered a crushing defeat by the tough Native Americans who had years of practice and experience! The next official game between them was not recorded until more than a hundred years later.

Today's version of the sport has evolved slightly, combining elements of hockey and rugby. All of today's lacrosse teams have ten players each, but

LAX RAT

when the Native Americans played the game, their teams had hundreds of people; even thousands of players were not uncommon. Games could last two or three days in a row, starting at dawn and ending at dusk. The modern-day game is much more formal with very specific rules and specialized equipment. It is not played on the countryside with poles, rocks, or trees serving

The Choctaws in what is now Oklahoma played lacrosse. As you can see from this painting, their games involved many, many players!

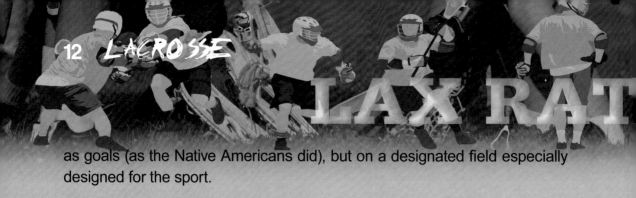

as goals (as the Native Americans did), but on a designated field especially designed for the sport.

White Settlers Take Up the Game

The white settlers officially adopted lacrosse in 1834 when a group of Montreal businessmen made arrangements for the Caughnawaga Indians to play in their city. From there, the popularity of the game quickly spread, and in 1851, a group of settlers finally succeeded in defeating a Native American team.

Montreal is known as the birthplace of modern lacrosse. The Montreal Lacrosse Club was formed in 1856, and immediate changes in rules and equipment followed. In 1867, Dr. W. George Beers, a dentist from Montreal who had founded the Canadian National Lacrosse Association, wrote the first official set of rules. Beer's rules included a limit on the number of players allowed per team and the requirements for playing field dimensions. In the same year, lacrosse was declared the official sport of the Dominion of Canada.

George Beers is known as the Father of Lacrosse because he wrote the first official rules.

Once established in Canada, lacrosse began to spread around the globe. In 1867, a Native American team toured England, Ireland, France, and Scotland; a year later, in 1868, the English Lacrosse Association was formed. In the United States, a group of Native Americans demonstrated the game at the Saratoga Springs fairgrounds in New York in 1867, which led to the creation of the first official lacrosse club in the country: the Mohawk Club of Troy. In 1874, lacrosse was introduced in Australia, and only four years later, it had spread to New Zealand. Intercollegiate lacrosse began in New York City at New York University. During the spring of 1881, Princeton and Columbia universities also formed lacrosse teams; Harvard, Yale, and Johns Hopkins universities soon followed. In 1882, Philips Andover Academy in Massachusetts, Philips Exeter Academy in New Hampshire, and the Lawrenceville School in New Jersey introduced the first high school lacrosse teams in the United States.

Since then, lacrosse has continued to grow and become more refined as a sport. In the United States alone, lacrosse is played at more than 500 colleges and universities, as well as more than 1,400 high schools. Little league and women's lacrosse teams now exist, and more than a hundred colleges and universities, along with 150 high schools, currently sponsor programs. Lacrosse was an official sport in the Olympic Games in 1904 and 1908, with Canada taking home the gold medal both times, but it was dropped from the games after that. It was reinstated as a demonstration sport in 1928, 1932, and 1948, and another exhibition tournament was held at the Olympics in Los Angeles in 1980.

The Rules of the Game

The sport of lacrosse has come a long way since the Native Americans first played it on the Canadian countryside. Today, it has very specific standards for equipment, field condition, and play.

The Legend of Lacrosse

According to a Cherokee myth, the animals once challenged the birds to a game of ball. The animals took positions on the ground, while the birds took positions in the trees to wait for the ball to be thrown up in the air.

As the birds watched the game, two small creatures climbed up the tree where the leader of the birds was waiting, and asked if they could join the game. Taking one look at these tiny creatures, the leader of the birds saw that they were four-footed and asked why they did not play on the animals' side, where they belonged. The creatures replied that they had already done so, but were laughed at and sent away because they were so small.

The leader of the birds felt sorry for the tiny creatures and wanted to let them play, but there was one problem: how could they join the birds' team when they had no wings? After discussing it, the birds decided to try and make wings for them. The leather head of a drum was cut up and used to make wings. These were attached to the legs of one of the creatures—and so the first bat was created.

The ball was tossed up, and the bat was told to catch it. His swiftness in dodging and circling about, keeping the ball con-

LAX RAT

stantly in motion and never letting it fall to the ground, soon convinced the birds that they had indeed made a wise decision.

They then turned their attention to the other little creature, but realized that the leather had been used up in making wings for the bat. The birds decided that stretching out the creature's skin might make wings. Two large birds seized him on each side with their strong bills and tugged and pulled at his fur until the skin between his front feet and his hind feet was stretched, and so the first flying squirrel was created. The leader of the birds threw the ball into the air, and the flying squirrel gracefully sprang off the limb to catch the ball in his teeth, and then sailed through the air to another tree a hundred feet away.

These two tiny creatures were so successful in dodging and flying, and keeping the ball out of the hands of even the fastest animals that they scored many goals for the birds, ultimately winning the game. In honor of their invaluable help, Cherokee players tie a small piece of a bat's wing to their lacrosse sticks for good luck.

THE TEAM

Each team has ten players: a goalkeeper, three defense, three midfielders, and three attacks. Each team must keep at least four players, including the goalie, in its defensive half of the field, and three in its offensive half. The midfielders may roam the entire field. There are no boundaries to the field (one of the only sports to have this rule), but play stops if the ball enters an area that is unplayable or not clearly visible to the official.

Offensive lacrosse players carry the ball downfield in the pocket of their stick, making sure to guard the ball from the other team's defense.

LAX RAT

PLAY

A game begins with the face-off: the ball is placed between the sticks of two players in the center of the field. At the whistle, the players fight for the ball until one of them has gained possession; only players in the wing areas may move. Players pass and catch the ball, and they may run with it in the stick. The only player whose hands may touch the ball is the goalkeeper.

THE BALL

A player may gain possession of the ball by dislodging it from an opponent's stick using a stick **check**, which includes the controlled poking and slapping of both the stick and the gloved hand of the player in possession of the ball. When the ball is grounded, covering it with the back of a stick's net and preventing play by another player is prohibited.

CHECKING

Body checking is permitted if the opponent has the ball. However, all contact must occur from the front or side, and be above the waist and below the shoulders. Checking is prohibited when it is directed toward the face, is too close to the head, is uncontrolled, or involves holding down another player's stick. An opponent's stick may also be checked if it is within 5 yards (4.5 m) of a loose ball or a ball in the air.

THE STICK

Before the game begins, the officials check every stick for legality. The most common illegality in a stick is that its pocket is too deep. The strings at the bottom of the stick's head can be pulled to tighten the pocket.

Careers in Lacrosse

For a career in lacrosse, you can choose to play professionally or become a coach. There are several ways these career goals can be accomplished.

Lacrosse

PROFESSIONAL LACROSSE PLAYER

When it comes to **professional** lacrosse teams, there are several leagues and organizations, including the Professional Lacrosse Players Association, the National Lacrosse League, and the Ontario Lacrosse Association; these leagues are often separated into geographical divisions. Although many other professional sports associations have existed for almost a century now, professional lacrosse is still in its infancy. According to Peter Schmitz, president of the Professional Lacrosse Players Association, things are changing, and he is confident that "this sport will become the next big sport in North America. It has all the ingredients that draw fan interest: games are high-scoring, physical, fast, action-packed, and skilled."

So how can you become a professional lacrosse player? For many young people, the path to becoming a professional lacrosse player begins in high school or college. Obviously, having some talent is a great benefit to the budding professional, but hard work, determination, and regular practice can go a long way. An average player may become a good player, and a good player can turn into a great one. The key to getting better is practice, practice, practice!

Legendary Lacrosse Players

On October 1, 2000, four Onondaga Nation residents were accepted posthumously into the U.S. Lacrosse Hall of Fame. Known as "The Fabulous Four," Oren Lyons, Lyle Pierce, Stanley Pierce, and Irving Powless supported the game of lacrosse and kept its traditions alive among their people. Of particular interest is the fact that they played against Johns Hopkins University in the tryouts for the Olympic games in 1932.

The goalie uses a special stick with a larger pocket in order to defend the goal from oncoming shots.

Becoming a professional lacrosse player will also mean finding a college that has a renowned or prestigious team. Many colleges offer lacrosse scholarships, and several, especially on the East Coast of the United States, have been known for decades for their outstanding collegiate lacrosse teams. Talk to your school's guidance counselor, visit the career center at your library, or talk to lacrosse coaches at the colleges you are considering in order to find out about available scholarships. Those that offer them include Johns Hopkins, Princeton, Rutgers, and the University of Maryland.

LAX RAT

Several colleges and universities offer scholarships for women's lacrosse, but unfortunately, there are currently no professional teams for women. Hopefully, as lacrosse continues to gain popularity, this will soon change. For women interested in pursuing a career in lacrosse, coaching a high school or college women's team is an option.

PROFESSIONAL LACROSSE COACH

A career as a professional lacrosse player can be relatively short, just like any other professional sport. Lacrosse puts enormous strains on the body and can cause permanent changes or injuries. Even players in the best of shape find that, sooner or later, their body has had enough. Sometimes, a player suffers an injury on the playing field that is so severe he is unable to continue playing professionally.

However, this does not mean that all careers in lacrosse are now out of the question. Often, those who played lacrosse in college or played professionally stay involved in the sport by becoming a coach. Furthermore, lacrosse coaches are needed for a wide range of ages, from middle school all the way up through college and into the pros, giving you many opportunities to stay involved and express your passion for the sport.

If you decide that you want to be a lacrosse coach, classes like **anatomy**, **physiology**, and physical education can be very helpful, because lacrosse coaches sometimes have to quickly assess and treat injuries on the field. In addition, consider getting a teaching certificate with a concentration in physical education, since many lacrosse coaches in schools and universities are also teachers or professors.

LAX RAT

C.O.A.C.H.

The acronym C.O.A.C.H. sums up the qualities of an effective lacrosse coach:

C—COMPREHENSION: An effective lacrosse coach thoroughly understands the ins and outs of the game and clearly communicates skills, rules, and game tactics to the players.

O—OUTLOOK: An effective lacrosse coach has a clear set of coaching objectives and goals. The most common ones are to have fun, to help players develop their physical, mental and social skills, and to win games (although winning is by no means the most important thing).

A—AFFECTION: An effective lacrosse coach has genuine care and concern for the health and welfare of the players and does not push them beyond their limits.

C—CHARACTER: An effective lacrosse coach knows the importance of being a good role model for players and strives always to treat everyone with respect and value.

H—HUMOR: An effective lacrosse coach always maintains a sense of humor, striving to make practices fun and enjoyable, and keeping players' mistakes in perspective.

2
Mental Preparation & Equipment

Understanding the Words

A **routine** is a repeated action that you do on a regular basis. The more you perform it, the more natural it will feel (for example, brushing your teeth, doing homework after school, or completing a daily exercise).

To **visualize** something is to make a mental image of it.

Etiquette is another word for good manners and behavior (acting appropriately during a game, for example, and presenting yourself well whether winning or losing).

To feel **optimism** is to believe or expect that something will turn out well, having a positive attitude or outlook about a situation.

A **concussion** is a head injury, usually a blow to the head that temporarily affects how your brain works. Memory, judgment, reflexes, speech, balance, and coordination are often affected. Concussions can be minor or major injuries.

Cleats are the shoes worn in outdoor sports, such as lacrosse, soccer, track, and football. There are tiny spikes on the bottom of the shoes to help grip the surface of the field to prevent sliding during play.

LACROSSE

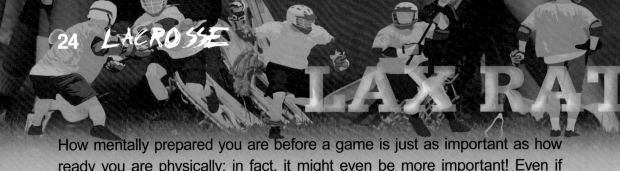

LAX RAT

How mentally prepared you are before a game is just as important as how ready you are physically; in fact, it might even be more important! Even if you have run through your team's plays a thousand times and are in peak physical condition, you will not succeed unless you have a confident, positive attitude.

That's why it is vital to have a **routine** where you **visualize** positive details of a game before it even begins. With your mind, you can create a vivid picture of what you want to happen: visualize yourself performing well technically without injury or mistake. For example, if you are concerned about an upcoming game in which you will be goalie, close your eyes and picture yourself blocking shot after shot. Then, when it comes to the actual game, the fact that you have rehearsed your athletic performance in your mind's eye allows you to have the confidence you need to give it your all.

Jack Nicklaus, former professional golfer, used visualization techniques throughout his entire career. Visualization helped him win the PGA tour a total of seventy-three times. He describes here how picturing success has made it a reality for him:

I never hit a shot, not even in practice, without having a very sharp, in-focus picture of it in my head. First I see the ball where I want it to finish, nice and white and sitting up high on the bright green grass. Then the scene quickly changes, and I see the ball going there; its path, trajectory, and shape, even its behavior on landing. Then there is a sort of fade-out, and the next scene shows me making the kind of swing that will turn the previous images into reality.

What worked for Jack Nicklaus on the golf course can work for you on the lacrosse field.

LAX RAT

Attitude

Attitude—the mindset with which you approach something—often makes the difference in your quality of play and even the outcome of a game. You should always try to maintain a positive attitude; there will be times that are more

In many cases, positive visualization can make the difference between a dropped pass and a game-making play.

LACROSSE

LAX RAT

Advice From Players

- Concentrate on having fun and on the game, no matter what.
- Approach the game as a goalie would: one shot at a time.
- Pay attention to the ball and talk to your teammates.
- Play the ball no matter who has it or where it is.
- Respect your opponents. Be polite and practice good **etiquette** at all times.
- Treat everyone—coaches, officials, teammates and opponents—with respect.

Source: www.LaxTips.com

difficult than others, such as a rough practice or a losing game, but keeping a good outlook can help you keep things in perspective.

Visualization can help in this area too. By visualizing what you want to achieve as a lacrosse player, your concentration and the determination to make your visions a reality can lead to an improved attitude. Sometimes pep talks by coaches or stories shared by other players can help you improve your **optimism** as well. No matter what, it is always important to stay focused: your teammates will be counting on you to give the game your full attention.

You should also bring an attitude of fun to any game or practice. Above all, sporting events are designed to be fun for players and spectators alike. Yes, you should take every game seriously, but winning or losing is less important than having fun and practicing good sportsmanship.

Equipment

The original game of lacrosse played by Native Americans was rather basic: players only needed a ball and a lacrosse stick. However, as the sport has become more standardized and complex, so has its equipment.

Men's lacrosse is traditionally rougher than women's, and helmets are required for all players. In women's lacrosse, only the goalie is required to wear a helmet, but it is an option for all players.

Just because helmets are not required, though, does not mean that women's lacrosse is not dangerous, or that precautions do not need to be taken. In fact, many studies show that many women injure themselves playing lacrosse. According to an article published by the Center for Neuro Skills,

Unlike the Native Americans who first played lacrosse—who played with only a ball and sticks—modern lacrosse players use a variety of special equipment created just for their sport, including sticks, helmets, gloves, pads, and team uniforms.

LAX RAT

"High rates of head and face injuries among women and the increasing numbers of children learning to play lacrosse . . . is prompting another look at how much protective gear they need." A second study, conducted by the

Only male lacrosse players must wear helmets, though it is an option for all female players. Goalies are the only female players who must wear a helmet at all times.

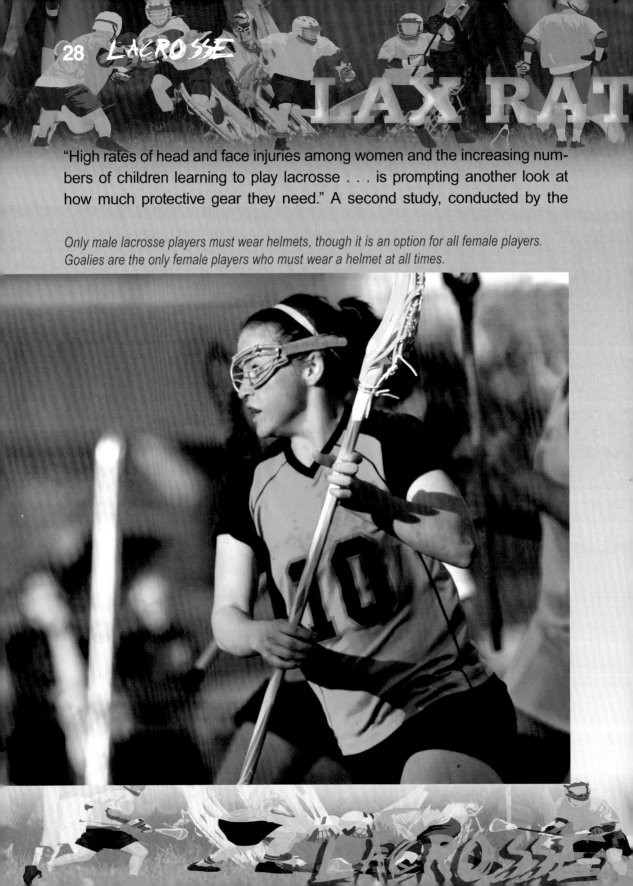

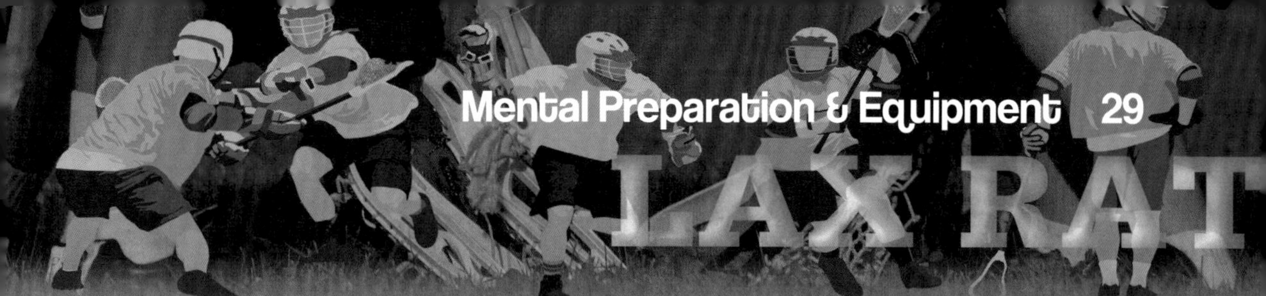

University of Virginia, discovered that "injuries to the head and face were significantly more prevalent among females (30.1 percent of all injuries) than among males (18 percent of all injuries), and often resulted from contact with the ball." Furthermore, "children ages four to eleven years old experienced the highest percent of injuries to the head and face of all lacrosse players."

Clearly, lacrosse is a game in which safety must be considered a priority. The following safety equipment is either recommended or required. Check with your coach or league to be sure of specific requirements.

MEN

- helmet with attached mouth guard
- rib, shoulder, and elbow pads
- padded gloves
- protective cup/jock strap
- shoes with cleats

WOMEN

- mouth guard
- padded gloves
- shoes with cleats

Female goalkeepers should also wear the following additional pieces of safety equipment:

- helmet with attached face guard, throat protector, and mouth guard
- chest protector
- arm and leg pads

LAX RAT

The strings that make up the pocket of each player's lacrosse stick can be tightened or loosened as the player wishes, but there are regulations preventing players from loosening the strings of the pocket so much that the ball cannot be knocked loose.

THE STICK

While guidelines and rules apply to players' sticks, the rules are not too specific. The "right" lacrosse stick is, ultimately, the one that is best for your age, sex, position, and abilities. For men, lacrosse sticks usually have aluminum handles with either a traditional or mesh pocket (a traditional pocket is made of nylon and leather; a mesh pocket consists of woven nylon webbing). The depth of the pocket can vary, and the typical length a men's lacrosse stick is 30–60 inches (76 cm to 1.5 m) depending on the position played and personal preference. For women, lacrosse sticks have either a wood or aluminum handle and a traditional pocket, which is shallower than the pocket used by men. The pocket of a woman's lacrosse stick has stricter regulations, requiring four or five leather thongs and more than two shooting strings. The typical length of a stick is 36–44 inches (.9–1.1 m).

THE HELMET

In general, lacrosse is an intense sport in which players are constantly checking each other and running the risk of injury from other player's sticks—so it only makes sense to wear a helmet. Ideally, a lacrosse helmet should provide full protection to the face and neck. Also, lacrosse face guards must meet certain standards. For example, the wire mesh of the guard must protect the face but not be too close to it. This prevents the guard from smashing into the player's face in the case of a head-on collision. In addition, the chinstrap must be padded to protect the face.

Mouth guards are usually attached directly to the helmet, but they can be sold separately as well. They serve to protect the teeth and cushion blows to the head, helping to prevent a **concussion**. Mouth guards come pre-formed, but eventually mold to the player's mouth with use over time.

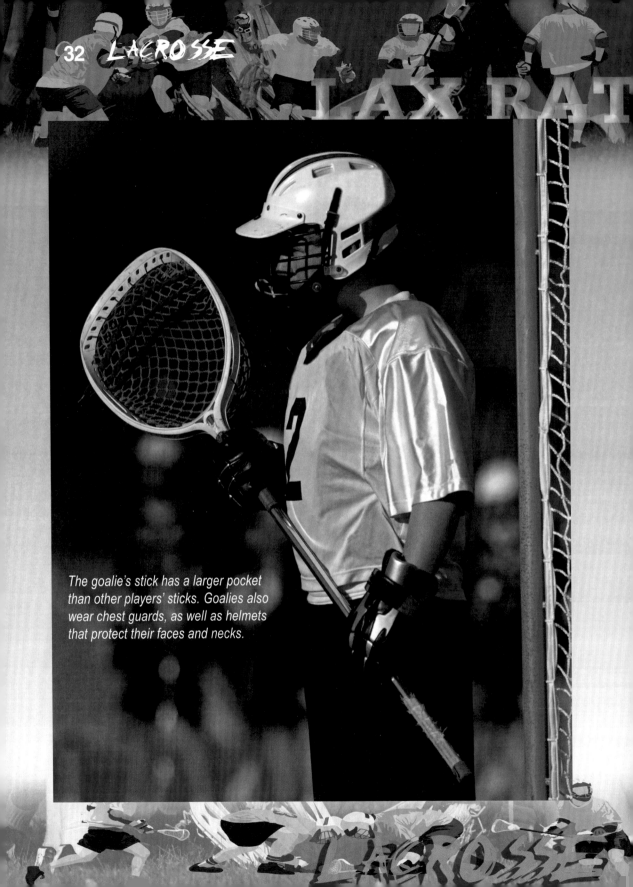

The goalie's stick has a larger pocket than other players' sticks. Goalies also wear chest guards, as well as helmets that protect their faces and necks.

SHOES

Lacrosse shoes are much the same for women and men. They are similar to a football or soccer shoe, in that they have **cleats**. Cleats enable players to get better traction on the field, but they can also cause severe injuries if the players are not careful. Long cleats provide better grip but can lead to knee injuries: if the foot becomes firmly planted in the ground, it can be ripped away too quickly with a twisting motion or impact from another player, forcing the knee joint beyond its normal range of motion. Be sure to choose a cleat that will benefit you on the field but will not endanger your safety.

GLOVES

Lacrosse gloves have heavy padding on the tops of the fingers and around the wrist to protect the hands from being hit by a stick. The palm is made of leather or a leather substitute, with thick pads around it for protection. Some players are known to cut the pads out of their gloves or purchase gloves without padding over the palms so that they can maintain a better grip on the stick. Do not do this without checking with your coach first.

To determine your glove size, use a tape measure to determine the distance from where your elbow pads will end to the tips of your fingers. This number equals your glove size, which will ensure that you get the gloves that fit you properly.

PADS

Lacrosse players wear lots of pads, primarily over the upper body. The goalie, in particular, needs to make sure that the pads are snug and comfortable.

Obviously, rib and shoulder pads are worn to protect the ribs and shoulders, as well as the kidney area. To determine your correct shoulder and rib pad size, wrap a tape measure around your chest just below your armpits. This will indicate the size of pads you need.

LAX RAT

Gloves should cover the forearm up to the shoulder pad so that no skin is exposed between the two pads.

Elbow pads serve to protect the elbow, of course, but also the upper arm and forearm areas. Many are secured with adjustable Velcro® straps. To determine your correct elbow pad size, measure the distance between the edge of your shoulder pads and the cuff of your lacrosse glove. Note that the

LACROSSE

LAX RAT

Maintenance

Safety equipment will do you no good if it is not well maintained. Regularly check all your equipment, from your shoes to your stick, for wear and tear, and replace or repair immediately anything that is worn out, damaged, or ill fitting.

You might also consider walking around the lacrosse field before you play, checking for holes or loose materials or debris. Anything unusual in the playing field should be brought to the attention of your coach or an official because it could present a hazard, not just to you but also to all the players on the field.

top of the elbow pad should leave no exposed skin between the shoulder pad and the glove.

Mental attitude and equipment are just two parts of the safety equation. Physical training is also vital, not only for skill and success on the lacrosse field but also for preparing your body for the demands of lacrosse.

3
Physical Preparation

Understanding the Words

*The part of the shoulder called the **rotator cuff** is made up of a group of muscles and tendons; these all work together to stabilize the shoulder while allowing your arm to turn.*

***Reaction time** is the amount of time it takes your mind and body to react to an outside stimulant (for example, how long it takes someone to duck or catch if a ball is thrown toward them).*

***Muscle memory** is the body's ability to memorize motor skills; this allows a person to perform an action without having to consciously think about doing it, as an automatic reaction (for example, riding a bike does not need to be relearned each time you do it).*

***Cardio** training involves longer periods of exercise at a medium intensity in order to increase your heart rate and oxygen intake and build your heart and lung strength.*

*Medial tibial stress syndrome, commonly referred to in sports as **shin splints**, is an injury in the shins caused by overused muscles from activities like running, jumping, or sprinting. Without proper healing time, shin splits can become more serious and turn into stress fractures in the bone.*

*A **centrifugal** force is a form of inertia that tries to pull something in a straight line away from a center axis. For example, the Earth tries to move in a straight line off into space, but the gravity from the sun keeps pulling it back, resulting in the Earth's orbit around the sun.*

LACROSSE

LAX RAT

When preparing to play "the fastest sport on two feet," it's extremely important to pay special attention to your body. During a typical college lacrosse game, each team takes seventy-five to eighty-five shots at the goals. For constant action like this, you need sharp reflexes and a body that can work quickly—and at the same time, you want to able to avoid injuries while playing.

Warming up before practice or playing a game is vital to avoiding injury. Stretching after a quick run or jog is a great way to start a warm-up routine.

LAX RAT

Warm-Up and Preconditioning

Even though warming up may seem like a hassle, it's just as important as the rest of your practices. Without properly warming up each and every muscle before a game, you risk pulling a muscle or seriously injuring yourself in another way. Stretches are a good way to get your muscles ready to perform.

When you are stretching, here are a few things you should keep in mind:

- Before stretching, run or jog lightly for a few minutes. This will help warm your muscles and allow for easier stretching; stretching a cold muscle is always more difficult.

- Each stretch should be held for a minimum of ten seconds. You can increase your flexibility by holding the stretches for longer periods of time—say twenty to thirty seconds.

- Do not bounce or jerk your muscles when you are stretching. While it may seem like you're helping to stretch out your muscles better, this can easily lead to tearing or spraining.

- Do not rush through stretching. This does your body no good and again, can lead to injury. Always take the time to warm up properly.

- Listen to your body and respect your limits. Gaining flexibility takes time; if something hurts excessively, stop right away. Don't be tempted to compare your stretching ability to anyone else's. Some bodies are naturally more flexible than others, and everyone has their own abilities and limits.

Here are some examples of stretches for different parts of the body.

LAX RAT

ibility. Hold for 15 seconds. You should feel this stretch in the backs of your knees and lower back. Try it with your toes pointing straight up and pointing forward.

• Sit with your legs spread wide apart. Lean over your left leg and grab your toes or left ankle. Point your toes forward, then back, and hold for another 15 seconds. Switch sides and perform this stretch over your right leg.

This stretch works the hamstrings, reducing the chances of injury.

Quadriceps

The quadriceps muscle, also known simply as a "quad," is a large group of four muscles that are found on the front of the thigh; it is the longest and leanest muscle in the human body.

• Stand with your feet shoulder-width apart. Grab your right ankle and pull it behind you toward your buttocks, bending your knee. You may need to hold onto a chair or wall for balance. Hold this stretch for 15 seconds and repeat with the left leg.

Practice this stretch to work your quads.

LAX RAT

Groin

- To perform what is known as the "butterfly stretch," sit on the floor with your knees bent and the soles of your feet pressed together. Hold your feet with your hands, then rest your elbows on your lower legs. Lean forward and try to touch your nose to the floor while you press down on your legs. Hold for 15 to 30 seconds.

Calves

- Stand facing a wall and place your hands at about shoulder height. Place one foot in front of the other, keeping the heel of your back foot planted firmly on the floor. Place your weight on your forward, bent leg, and then lean forward, as if you were trying to push against the wall. Hold for 15 seconds and repeat with the other leg.

- For this second calf stretch, you will need a flight of stairs or a sturdy box. First, line up your heels with the edge of the step. Then, move your feet back so that the balls of your feet are on the edge of the step and the rest of your feet are hanging off the edge. Slowly dip your heels down and come back up. Repeat ten times.

Ankles

Stand with your legs shoulder-width apart. Point your right toe so that it touches the ground, and roll your ankle in a clockwise direction three times. Then roll the ankle counterclockwise three times. Repeat with the left foot.

Training and Conditioning

Every sport requires specific talents and skills—and it also requires certain training to sharpen these skills.

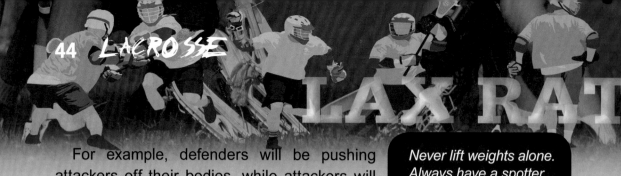

LAX RAT

For example, defenders will be pushing attackers off their bodies, while attackers will be using pushing motions when facing off and also to secure elbowroom and move around in a crush. Both will need strong triceps and strong pectorals, which are the thick muscles of the chest. Also called "pecs" for short, these are the thick muscles on the chest. They make up the bulk of the chest muscles in males and lie under the breasts in females.

Never lift weights alone. Always have a spotter standing over you as you lift the weight to make sure you don't accidentally drop it on yourself, and so the weight can be lifted back onto the bar if you are too tired to continue.

PECS

To perform an inclined press, lie on a weight bench that is at an angle; your shoulders should be higher than your buttocks. The weight bar should be supported on rests at a level with your chest. Grasp the weight bar with both hands and lift the weight over your forehead and then back to your chest. Repeat as many times as possible, working up to a higher number each time.

ABDOMINALS

For all players, regardless of position, strong abdominals are a must. Crunches are the most basic (and effective) way to enhance this area.

Oblique crunches work the oblique muscles, which are on the sides of your abdominals. To perform them, lie on your back with your knees bent and your feet on the floor, with hands behind your head. Next, twist your legs to the right and lower your knees to the floor. With your lower body in this position, raise your upper body so your shoulders do not touch the floor, then slowly lower back down. Repeat ten to twenty times, then repeat the set. Then twist your legs to the left and repeat the crunching movement on the right side of the body.

LACROSSE

LAX RAT

This young man is doing an inclined press to build his pecs.

LACROSSE

A lighter dumbbell can be used to strengthen your wrists. Strong wrists are important for stick work.

SHOULDERS

The shoulders are also a very essential part of lacrosse; with so much stick work, facing off, shooting, and checking, this body part can take a beating after just one or two games. Also, strong shoulder muscles can definitely help prevent rotator cuff injuries.

The military press is a great exercise for developing the shoulders. Hold a set of 5 to 10 pound (2.3–4.5 kg) dumbbells at shoulder height with your palms facing forward. Raise the dumbbells above your head, twisting your hand at the same time, so at the end of the movement, your palms are facing each other over the top of your head. Then lower the weights back to shoulder level, twisting again so that the palms are facing forward. Perform this action ten to fifteen times.

Also important for stick work is the condition of your wrists. Although this is a part of the body we often overlook, our wrists can be injured just like any other muscle. A great strengthening exercise is the wrist curl: Sit in a chair with your knees bent. Hold a 1 to 3 (.5–1.4 kg) pound dumbbell in one hand, palm down, with your forearm on your thigh. Slowly bend your wrist upward as far as possible. Hold for 10 to 20 seconds, then lower the wrist slowly, keeping your forearm on your thigh. Repeat ten times, and then switch to the other hand.

Next, hold the dumbbell with your palm face down and your forearm on your thigh. Slowly bend the wrist as far as possible and hold for 10 to 20 seconds, and then lower slowly. Repeat ten times, and then repeat with the other hand.

PLYOMETRICS

Another vital part of your workout routine should be plyometrics, or "plyos," as they are commonly called. This form of exercise is designed to train your body to produce fast, powerful movements, and improve functions like reaction time and muscle memory. When you are on the field in the last few minutes of a game, you may only have a split second to get your body moving and make a decision; you will not have the time to stop and think about what you will do or how to perform a move. Instead, with enough training, your body will automatically take over and perform the correct way.

The following plyometrics exercise is specific to lacrosse and was designed by Michael R. Rankin, the head strength and conditioning coach at Drexel University. (As always, be sure to consult your trainer or coach before beginning a program; this is an example of the types of training you should be doing with your coach and fellow teammates.)

Water, Water, Water

When you are playing a sport, you sweat, losing water. As a result, your body becomes dehydrated. Dehydration can seriously affect your athletic performance: you may tire faster and have less stamina, and your muscles may feel weak. Drink plenty of water during breaks between warm-ups and games, to make sure that your body stays properly hydrated.

Of course, drinking plenty of water is even more important when you are playing in hot or humid weather. During warm weather, cool water is a better choice for you than freezing cold or warm water. Drinking very cold water may cause your muscles to cramp: your already tired muscles will have to make a sudden effort to warm up the water. As for warm fluids, these are absorbed less quickly than cool water, and cool water itself is more likely to help cool off your overheated body.

LAX RAT

Types of Dodges

- A face dodge is used when you are being rushed at head-on by another player.
- A roll dodge is used when another player is trying to swing at or check your stick.
- The bull dodge is used when another player is standing still.

- *Depth jump with blocking pad or with pass catching:*

  Stand on a box 12–42 inches (30 cm to 1 m) high, toes close to the edge with stick in hand. Have a partner or coach stand facing the box, about four feet away from you with a blocking pad, or, have a partner stand about 5–10 yards (4.6–9.2 m) away ready to pass. Step off the box and land on both feet. Upon landing, explode into the blocking bag shoulder first. If receiving a catch, upon landing jump forward and catch the ball. For female players, always practice this routine by catching a ball. Complete five sets with five repetitions.

- *30-60-90 box drill:*

  Stand beside a 12–20 inch (30–51 cm) box with feet shoulder width apart. Jump onto the box and back down to the ground on the opposite side, continuing back and forth across the box. Do thirty repetitions of one, two, or three, depending on your endurance level (making 30, 60, or 90 jumps total.)

CARDIO TRAINING

During both preseason and your playing season, the training schedule that your coach sets up for you and your teammates will without a doubt include

LACROSSE

LAX RAT

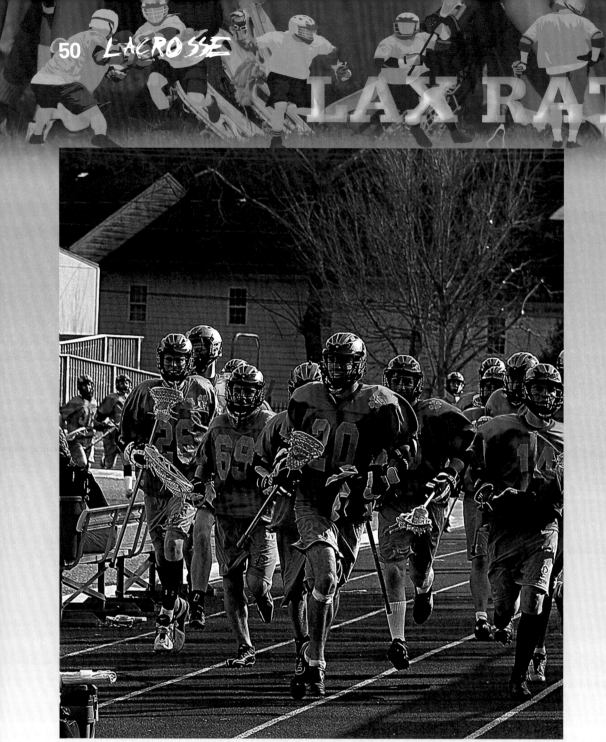

Running is part of this lacrosse team's training, improving their stamina during games.

LAX RAT

cardio. In order to improve stamina and endurance during a game, your body must be in physical shape to keep moving continuously for long periods without breaks. Although you will be running quite a bit during practice, your coach might suggest you run or do other exercises outside of formal practice to amp up your conditioning. Something as simple as going for a 30- to 60-minute run on days that you don't have practice can improve your stamina—but be sure not to overdo it. Too much running done too suddenly can be extremely hard on the body, and it can contribute to injuries such as **shin splints**. Always be sure you have the proper shoes, and if possible, run on a softer surface like grass, as opposed to pavement.

DRILLS

Drills are a series of exercises designed to build specific skills geared toward a sport or position. For example, basketball players will not necessarily practice with the same drills that lacrosse players do, nor will a goalie need to know all of the tactics that an attack does, and vice versa. In lacrosse, drills are designed to help players develop better ball handling, stick handling, and eye-hand coordination, a crucial skill to have in this sport. There are also drills based on individual positions.

Drills for Offense

- This first offensive drill builds the skill of cradling, which refers to the movement of the stick in a semicircular pattern, which creates a **centrifugal** force that keeps the ball in the pocket of the stick. This drill is popularly known as "Rock-a-Bye-Baby." Sit on the ground cross-legged and hold the stick with the top hand just below the pocket and the other hand halfway down the shaft of the stick. Extend the stick at an angle of about 45° away from the body. Rock the ball from side to side, like you are rocking a baby, moving not more than 12 inches (30 cm) in total—in other words, about 6 inches (15 cm) to each side.

LACROSSE

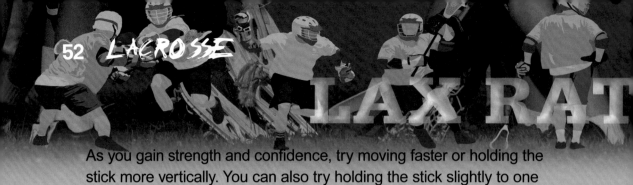

As you gain strength and confidence, try moving faster or holding the stick more vertically. You can also try holding the stick slightly to one side of the body and repeating the rocking motion.

• The next drill develops your skills in passing, for which you will need a partner. Begin by standing about 30 feet (9 m) apart from one another. Pass the ball back and forth, concentrating on maintaining the proper form when catching and throwing. As a variation, you can practice catching with your non-dominate hand: for example, if you are right-handed, try throwing and catching with your left hand. Or you can throw with your right and catch with your left.

• A third drill works on your skills in dodging—the sudden change in movement of the stick and ball in an effort to keep it away from an opponent. For this drill, you need four to six lacrosse players. Everyone should stand in a line, with one person standing about 15 feet (4.5 m) from the line of other players. This person is the one with the ball. To start, the person in front calls out the type of dodge she intends to execute, then runs down the line of players, weaving in and out while performing dodges until the end of the line is reached. At this point, the ball is given to the player at the end of the line, who moves in front of the row, calls out the intended dodge, and moves through the line. This pattern continues until everyone has had a turn

• This last offensive drill develops scooping, which is exactly what it sounds like: scooping up the loose ball and returning it to play on the field. For this drill, you will need another player. Stand facing each other, about 30 feet (9 m) apart. Start with the ball at your feet. Scoop it up, and then pass it to your partner. Concentrate on maintaining the proper form for both scooping and catching. After catching the ball, your partner should run a few steps and then pass the ball back to

LAX RAT

you. Take turns starting with the ball at each other's feet. For a variation, try scooping with your non-dominate hand or alternate between both of them.

Drills for Defense

• This first defensive drill works on the skill of body checking (when you, as a defender, move in the same direction as the person who is carrying the ball, with your body positioned in such a way that it blocks the player from moving in the direction he wants to go). In this drill, you will need a partner and a space about 30 feet (9 m) wide and 60 feet (18 m) long. One person starts with the ball. At the beginning of the 60-foot mark, this person should run the length of this area. The partner, who is acting as the defender, should follow, running alongside and concentrating on maintaining proper body position and footwork at the same time. The defender should try to remain on only one side of the ball carrier the entire time. Take turns being the ball carrier and the defender.

• Footwork is an important skill in lacrosse, especially in defensive positions. You will need coordination as you run around the field, passing and catching the ball, but you will also have to focus on dodging and checking other players. The following drill is aimed at building your fundamental footwork skills: Place your lacrosse stick on the ground, horizontally in front of you. Step over the stick with one foot, then the next. Then, step backward with the second foot, and follow with the first. The movement should feel like you are running in place over your stick. Concentrate on keeping your knees high. After a few minutes of this, squat down slightly keeping the stick in front, and slide to the side of the stick. Step forward so you are in front of it, and then slide to the other side of the stick and step back behind it.

LAX RAT

This causes you to perform a sliding motion around the stick. Then, with the stick vertical in front of you, jump over it with both feet, and then jump back to the other side. Continue jumping back and forth for a few minutes, making sure that your knees are lifted high in the air when you jump. Finally, take several lacrosse sticks, cones, or whatever you can find that is handy, and place the objects in two lines, about 1 foot (30 cm) apart. Step forward between the objects with your knees as high as possible. This drill should feel and look a lot like the drill you see football players performing when they run along a row of tires, placing each foot in the middle of the tire.

• The next drill works on stick checking, the repeated tapping motion a defender uses to dislodge the ball from an opponent's stick. This drill, known as "Woody Woodpecker," helps teach the motion and control necessary for stick checking. You will need a partner for this exercise. One person should hold her stick horizontal to the ground, anywhere from hip to shoulder level, and the other person should hit the "opponent's" stick with her stick, using firm and rapid motions, like a woodpecker tapping on a tree. Try this in different positions, such as behind, forward, and to each side. When done, switch roles and repeat.

• The final defensive drill is a blocking drill known as "Monkey in the Middle." You will need two other people to practice this drill. They should stand facing each other about 30 feet (9 m) apart. As the first person throws the ball to the second person, the person in the middle (the "monkey") should attempt to block the pass. If the monkey is successful in this attempt, the monkey takes possession. If unsuccessful, the monkey must quickly run around the first person and then head

LAX RAT

for the second person, trying to block the shot again. Basically, it's a game of keep-away. Be sure to take turns alternating the position of "monkey."

Proper training combined with the right attitude and the right equipment goes a long way toward preventing injuries on the lacrosse field. No matter how carefully you prepare, however, sometimes injuries happen. When they do, it's important to know how to recover as quickly as possible, so you can get back on the field.

4
Common Injuries, Treatment, & Recovery

Understanding the Words

A **fracture** *is simply another term for a broken bone.*

Dislocations *occur when a force separates two bones that meet at a joint.*

Something that is **immobile** *is unable to move.*

A **splint** *is a rigid device that is used to hold a body part in place and promote healing.*

Mobility *is the ability to move.*

Ligaments *are fibrous, slightly stretchy connective tissues that hold one bone to another, forming a joint.*

An **overuse injury** *is an injury caused by a repeated motion over a long period of time that puts a strain on a particular body part.*

A **contusion** *is another name for a bruise.*

Involuntary muscle contractions are known as **spasms**. *They occur suddenly but go away quickly, and are usually painful.*

An injury that is **debilitating** *is one that weakens and impairs ability.*

Compression *is the physical application of pressure to an injury.*

Tendons *are the stretchy tissues that connect muscles to bones.*

Cartilage *is a rubbery material found in joints and in your ears and nose.*

LACROSSE

LAX RAT

Because lacrosse is a contact sport similar to hockey and rugby, the potential for injury is similar as well. A proper warm-up, like those discussed in the last chapter, can help prevent injuries—but despite all precautions, injuries still sometimes occur. In lacrosse, the specific areas of injury include hands and wrists, shoulders, thighs, and knees.

Hand and Wrist Injuries

Injuries to the hand and wrist suffered by lacrosse players include fractures, dislocations, and sprains. These can occur as a result of a player falling to the ground, getting hit on the head by another player's stick, or colliding with another player.

Typically, a fracture is not something you can treat yourself. Until you can consult a physician, the usual treatment is to keep the injured area immobile and apply an ice pack for twenty to thirty minutes. According to Dr. Allan M. Levy, team physician for the New York Giants football team, "many finger fractures are not serious, especially those in the tip of the finger. . . . Taping an injured finger to the healthy one next to it usually allows you to return to activity. " However, Dr. Levy, who is known as a father of sports medicine, also notes that if the fracture occurs in the second or third finger bone, a splint may be required in which case it can take four to six weeks for the fracture to heal completely.

A finger may be dislocated if it is struck with a great deal of force, either by a player or a player's equipment. Common symptoms can include pain, a loss of mobility in the finger, and a noticeable deformity in the joint. Do not try to force the joint back into place yourself—you can potentially cause more damage. Instead, Dr. Levy recommends that you tape the dislocated finger to the healthy one next to it and ice the area for periods of twenty to thirty minutes. Consult a physician to arrange for X-rays as soon as possible. These will determine the severity of the injury and establish whether there

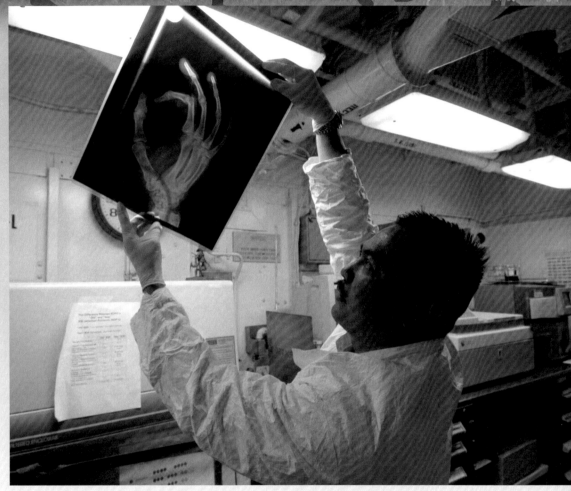

This X-ray reveals a broken finger.

are fractures. Typically, you will have to wear a splint to immobilize the joint. Usually, recovery time is anywhere from six to twelve weeks.

A sprain occurs when **ligaments** are stretched or torn. Finger sprains can occur when a lacrosse player receives a blow to the end of a finger or if the

Minor Injuries

Cuts

- Grab the cleanest material you can find, such as a wash-cloth or a strip of gauze.
- Cover the cut with the cloth, and apply firm pressure to the wound. Maintain this pressure until the bleeding has stopped.
- Next, clean the wound gently with an antiseptic and spread a thin layer of antibiotic ointment over the wound.
- If you cannot control the bleeding within a few minutes, seek medical help.

Bruises

- Apply a cold compress or ice pack to the bruised area as soon as possible. Leave in place for fifteen minutes. Repeat at twenty-minute intervals over a period of at least four hours until swelling has stopped.

Sprains

- Apply a cold compress or ice pack as soon as possible. Leave in place for fifteen minutes. Repeat at twenty-minute intervals over a period of at least four hours until swelling has stopped.
- Elevate the sprained limb to at least waist level to help alleviate swelling.
- Once the swelling has stopped, soak the sprained area three times a day—first in warm water for twenty minutes, then in icy water for twenty.

LAX RAT

finger joints are forced beyond their normal range of motion, which might happen if a player falls to the ground or bumps against another player with great force. Typical symptoms include pain, swelling, and loss of mobility. This is not something that you should treat by yourself. Keep the joint immobile by taping it to a healthy finger and apply ice for twenty-minute intervals until you can consult a physician. In most cases, treatment may consist of keeping the finger in a splint for two weeks. After that, it will be taped to a healthy finger until the injury is completely healed and full mobility is restored.

Lacrosse is a sport in which players often have to perform quick "snap-and-twist" motions when they quickly catch the ball and throw it to another player. As a result, a common wrist injury that players can suffer is a strain brought about by simple overuse.

Shoulders

Shoulder injuries can be common in lacrosse players, primarily for two reasons. First, shoulder injuries are often **overuse injuries** and can occur as a result of the constant twisting and throwing motions that players engage in during the course of a game. Second, shoulder injuries are also common due to players being struck with a lacrosse stick or landing heavily if they fall to the ground.

Common shoulder injuries often seen in lacrosse players include fractures, dislocations, sprains, and **contusions**. Fractures in the shoulder area almost always affect the collarbone, usually in the middle. A lacrosse player might suffer a fractured collarbone by receiving a direct hit to it, falling on it, or falling with outstretched arms. A fractured collarbone is a serious injury. If you suspect such an injury, keep the arm still: immobilize it in a sling, and wrap a bandage around the arm so that it is kept close to the body. Ice may be applied for twenty-minute intervals until a doctor can be seen. Typical recovery time is anywhere from six to twelve weeks.

LACROSSE

LAX RAT

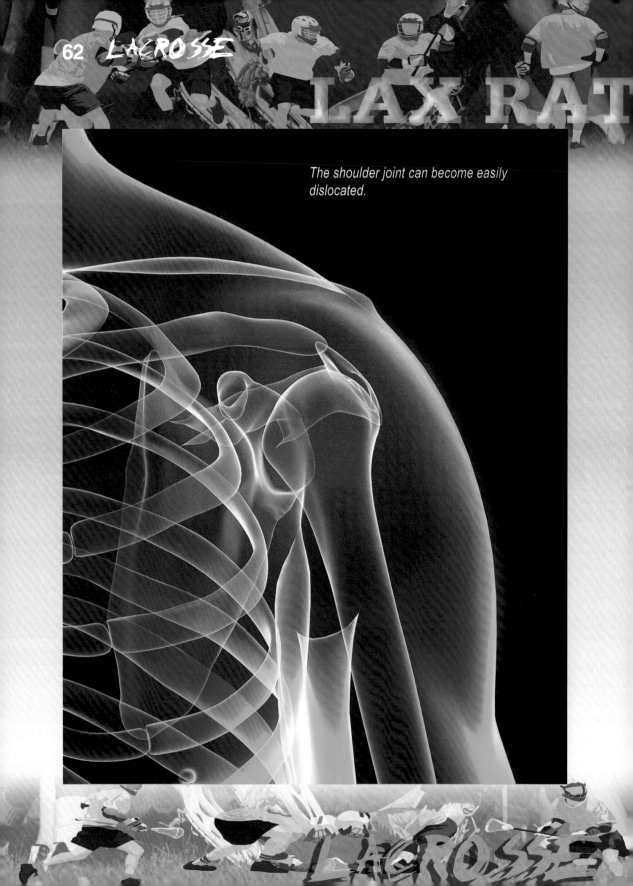

The shoulder joint can become easily dislocated.

LACROSSE

The shoulder is unique in that it is a shallow ball-and-socket joint, which means that the joint is not very stable. According to Dr. Levy, the shoulder is the only joint in the body that is not held together by its ligaments. Rather, the few ligaments serve only to keep it from moving too far in any one direction. For that very reason, shoulder dislocations are common among lacrosse players. If the ball at the top of the upper arm bone comes out of the socket in the shoulder blade, symptoms include an obvious deformity of the shoulder, extreme pain, muscle **spasms**, and loss of mobility. You should not try to force the shoulder joint back in place or have anyone else try to do it for you. Instead, place your arm in a sling and ice the affected area for twenty-minute intervals, until you can consult a doctor.

These shoulder injuries are often caused by accidents, which, by definition, are difficult to prevent. The most important safety measure is to learn how to fall properly. Too often, when a person falls, the natural reaction is to hold out the arms in order to break the fall. This action, though, can lead to the very shoulder injuries just described. Instead, tuck in and roll with the fall rather than trying to break it. Your lacrosse coach or your doctor should be able to give you further instruction in this area. Shoulder pads are also a good way to lessen the impact of a fall or blow to the shoulder.

Thighs

Common thigh injuries suffered by lacrosse players can include strains, bruises, and fractures. Particularly common are injuries to the hamstring and quadriceps.

The hamstring causes the knee to bend and the thigh to move backward relative to the body. Hamstrings play a vital role in walking, running, jumping, and controlling movement. A hamstring strain is one of the most common injuries and one of the most **debilitating**, because it is such a large muscle

What People Say About Lacrosse

Oren Lyons, Jr., a Native American and former college lacrosse player:

> "When you talk about lacrosse, you talk about the life-blood of the Six Nations. The game is ingrained into our culture and our system and our lives."

> "There are two times of the year that stir the blood. In the fall, for the hunt, and now for lacrosse."

Coleen Taylor, High school girls' lacrosse coach:

> "Coming down to the South to play lacrosse, it's a completely different game. Lacrosse is so new here and fresh. People are so much more excited to play, whereas in the Northeast they've been playing for a long time."

group. Typical symptoms of a hamstring pull can include sharp pain and swelling, and, in the most severe tears, bruising due to internal bleeding within the muscle. You may also be unable to raise your leg straight off the ground more than a short distance without feeling pain. Typical treatment includes rest, ice, and compression; usually, resting for at least two or three days; icing the muscle for twenty minutes, three to four times a day; and wrapping the muscle in a compression bandage.

Symptoms of a quadriceps injury include a sudden, stabbing pain in the front of the thigh; tenderness or possible discoloration on the front of the

LAX RAT

Jim Jennings, former National Lacrosse League Commissioner:

"They don't get paid a lot, but they [lacrosse players] are the best at what they do. The way they juggle their personal lives with lacrosse. . . . You have to have strong mental skills as well as strong physical skills to play in this league."

Gary Husmann:

"In another 10 years, lacrosse will be what everybody's kids are playing."

Aaron Gray, college lacrosse player:

Lacrosse is fast paced and I like fast-paced games. It's demanding physically and has the hardest conditioning of any sport. You are always running if you are not sprinting. It's constant movement.

thigh; and pain when trying to straighten the knee. Typical treatment includes resting the injury for several days, icing to reduce swelling, wearing a compression bandage, then a gentle muscle stretching program to strengthen the muscles.

The Knee

The knee is a complex joint, an intricate network of muscle, tendons, ligaments, cartilage, and bone, which assists us in a variety of motions. Knee

LAX RAT

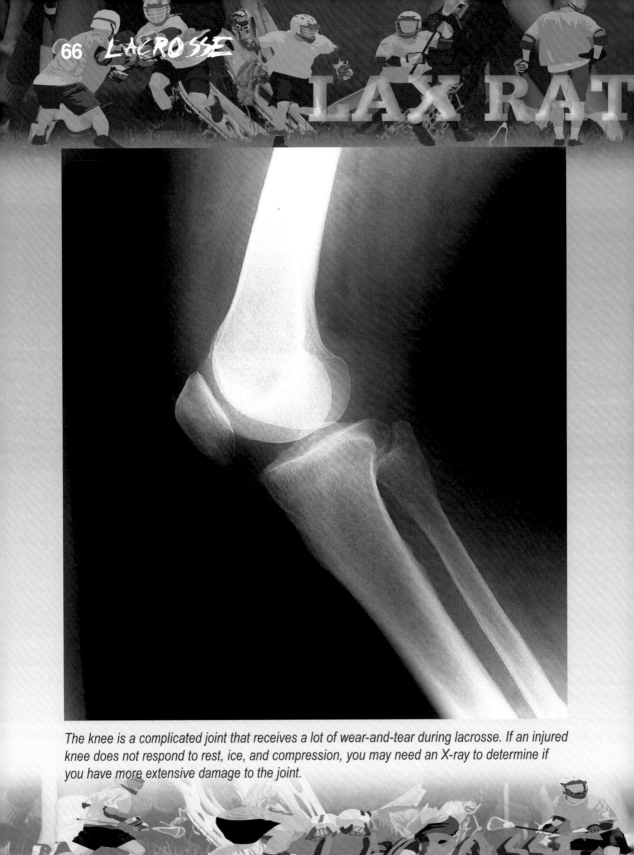

The knee is a complicated joint that receives a lot of wear-and-tear during lacrosse. If an injured knee does not respond to rest, ice, and compression, you may need an X-ray to determine if you have more extensive damage to the joint.

sprains are among the most common knee injuries seen in lacrosse players, and the recommended method of treatment is the familiar routine of resting, icing, and compressing the knee.

Keep in mind that the information in this chapter is not intended to replace the advice of your coach or physician.

5
Nutrition and Supplements

Understanding the Words

A **nutritionist** *is an expert in nutrition; she can help you put together a healthy diet that is right for your body's needs.*

To **synthesize** *means to put together, to make.*

If something is **fortified,** *it has been made stronger (or more nutritious) than normal.*

LAX RAT

Although practice and training are an important part of being safe and successful in the game of lacrosse, it is also important to pay attention to what foods you are consuming. Athletes must be careful to eat a proper blend of nutrients to make sure their bodies and minds perform as well as they possibly can. This doesn't just mean eating healthy foods but also choosing when to eat, how much to eat, and whether to take dietary supplements. Of course, when you choose a new diet or supplement, you should consult with a nutritionist, doctor, or some other expert. Don't make up your own nutrition program!

What to Eat

While a balanced diet is important for everyone, it is even more important for athletes. Typically, an athlete has to eat considerably more than other people

Including plenty of vegetables in your diet is important for everyone, but particularly for athletes who are placing higher demands on their bodies.

LAX RAT

do in order to maintain higher energy levels. The United States Food and Drug Administration (FDA) suggests that the average American should eat about 2,000 calories a day; for a male high school-or college-level athlete, a 3,000–4,000 calorie diet is more common. There are three main food groups to consider when choosing a diet: carbohydrates, protein, and fats.

CARBOHYDRATES

Carbohydrates are foods rich in a chemical called starch, which is what the body breaks down to get energy. Starchy foods include breads and grains, cereal, pasta, rice, and vegetables such as potatoes. Roughly half an athlete's calories should come from carbohydrates, but you should beware of heavily processed carbohydrates such as sugary foods and white bread made with bleached flour. These foods are quickly broken down into sugars, which the body processes into fats if it does not immediately burn them off. The best

Staying Hydrated

The best diet in the world is no good if you become dehydrated. Dehydration occurs when your body doesn't have enough water, leading to fatigue, dizziness, and headaches, all of which can hurt your performance when playing. It's best to carry a bottle of water with you the whole day before a practice or game to make sure you are fully hydrated. In addition, you should be drinking water throughout the game to avoid becoming dehydrated as you sweat; staying fully hydrated has many benefits. Besides helping your performance in a game, it can help concentration, improve digestive health, and reduce the risk of kidney stones.

LACROSSE

carbohydrate choices for an athlete are pasta and whole-grain foods, as well as starchy vegetables, which have vitamins as well as carbohydrates. A balanced diet avoids the "empty calories" supplied by white bread and sugars.

PROTEINS

Proteins are important chemicals found in all living things; these chemicals are used to perform specific functions inside our body cells. Each protein is a long, folded chain-like molecule made up of "links" called amino acids. Our bodies can break down proteins into their base amino acids and use them to build new proteins that make up our muscles and bones. For this reason, it is important to eat enough protein to give the body the building blocks it needs to become stronger, especially during exercise. The best sources of protein are meat and dairy products such as milk or cheese, as well as eggs and certain vegetables (like soy and beans). To know how much protein to eat, a good rule of thumb is that the number of grams should be equal to about

Cholesterol

A lot of bad things have been said about cholesterol—but most of this bad press focuses on LDLs, or low-density lipoproteins, a kind of cholesterol that can clog our blood vessels and make our hearts work harder. Our bodies make this cholesterol out of saturated fats, like those found in animal fat from meats, butter, and whole milk. It is important to know, though, that there is a kind of cholesterol that has a good effect on the body. HDLs, or high-density lipoproteins can be increased as easily as exercising regularly.

LAX RAT

one-third of your body weight in pounds. For example, a 200-pound person should have roughly 70 grams of protein per day.

FATS

Lots of times we think of fats as strictly "bad," since eating too much of them is unhealthy. However, fat is an important ingredient needed to make our bodies function correctly. Without fats, we could not absorb certain vitamins efficiently. Our skin and hair also need some amount of fat in order to grow correctly. However, fats should still be eaten in moderation—no more than 70 grams per day. The best sources of fat are vegetable oils, olive oil, and nuts.

Low-fat yogurt is a good high-protein snack option. Eating protein after a game or practice helps your muscles repair themselves more quickly.

LACROSSE

Many foods contain saturated fats, which lead to the formation of cholesterol and can force your heart to work harder.

Dietary Supplements

Many athletes seek to improve their performance by taking dietary supplements—pills or drinks that contain nutrients or chemicals—to improve their performance during the game. Dietary supplements do not include illegal performance-enhancing drugs. Instead, they contain vitamins, minerals, or chemicals that help the body use those vitamins more efficiently. When properly used, supplements can improve overall health and performance, but you should always consult a doctor or nutritionist before taking them. Some examples of common supplements include vitamin tablets, creatine, and protein shakes or powder.

VITAMIN TABLETS

We do not always get the vitamins and nutrients we need, usually because our diets are not as balanced as they should be. Sometimes, it's because the foods available to us have been processed in such a way that they lose their nutrients. Also, exhausted soil all over the country means that fruits and vegetables are often not as nutrient-rich as they should be. In many cases, we can get vitamins we need from vitamin supplements. These supplements, usually taken as pills, contain a balanced mixture of vitamins and nutrients known as multivitamins. Sometimes they contain a single vitamin or mineral that our diet is lacking. Be careful when taking vitamin supplements, however, because it is possible to overdose on certain ones. Don't assume that more is always better! And don't forget to always talk to your doctor before beginning supplements of any kind.

LAX RAT

CREATINE

Creatine is a specific protein naturally found in your body's muscle cells. When taken in larger doses than is found in the body, creatine has the effect of increasing the rate of protein **synthesis** within your body's cells. You will have more energy to exercise, and you will see a greater improvement in strength and speed when you do. However, putting any chemical into your

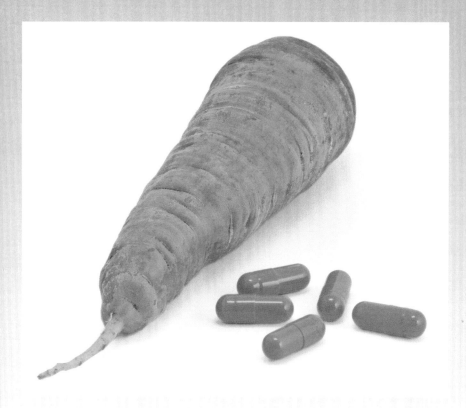

It's always better to get your vitamins from vegetables and other foods, rather than from pills— but since many of us fail to eat a completely balanced diet, vitamin pills can help us to make up the difference.

LACROSSE

body can have negative effects, and you should talk to a doctor before starting creatine. Creatine is only suited for adult athletes, though, so young people under the age of seventeen should not take it.

If you're going to drink alcohol, don't do so during the lacrosse season. Most high school teams have rules against drinking. There are good reasons for these rules, since alcohol interferes with your physical performance during games and slows recovery from injuries.

LAX RAT

Lacrosse and Alcohol

After a big victory, players may be tempted to celebrate with alcohol. They may also be tempted to use it to ease the pain of defeat. But alcohol intake can interfere with the body's recovery process, and this may interfere with your next game's performance. It's especially important to avoid any alcohol 24 hours after exercise if you have any soft tissue injuries or bruises. Alcohol and injuries are a bad combination, as alcohol can increase swelling and bleeding, delaying the healing process.

PROTEIN SUPPLEMENTS

Eating protein immediately after a workout is recommended in order to refuel your body, because protein helps build and repair muscles. Getting enough protein from the food you eat, however, can be difficult. Not many people feel like preparing a meal right after exercising, so protein shakes are often a convenient and healthy choice. Many shakes contain blends of protein, carbohydrates, and fats, and some include vitamins to help balance an athlete's diet. You should always remember, however, that while protein shakes are useful for supplementing your diet, they should never be used to replace meals in significant quantities. Your body still needs plenty of nutrients that it can only get from a balanced diet. No matter how **fortified** a protein shake may be, it cannot adequately replace a real meal. A nutrition-ist can tell you how to fit protein or supplement shakes into your diet safely and effectively.

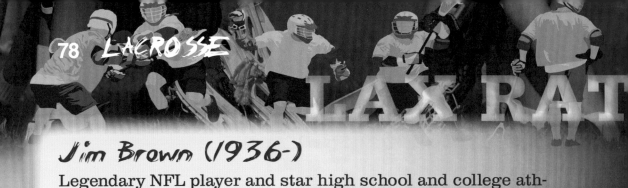

Jim Brown (1936–)

Legendary NFL player and star high school and college athlete Jim Brown excelled in every sport he tried—but he started out his sporting career playing lacrosse. Jim Brown was the greatest all-around athlete in Syracuse University's history, succeeding in four different sports (basketball, football, lacrosse, and track). He once competed in two sports on the same day. In May 1957, he participated in the track meet, won the high jump and discus, and helped Syracuse beat Colgate that day. The same day, he put on his lacrosse uniform and led the way to a win over Army, completing Syracuse's undefeated season.

Even though he was a legend specifically in football at Syracuse, Brown is, to this day, considered one of the greatest lacrosse players of all time. During his senior season in college, he led Syracuse to an undefeated team and was co-leader of the national scoring championship. Jim Brown's incredible athleticism and technique helped put lacrosse into the mainstream in the 1950s.

After being a successful lacrosse, baseball, and basketball player, track star, college boxer, and professional football player for nine seasons (named MVP four times), Brown managed to retire at the age of thirty and become active in even more endeavors. He pursued his dream of being an actor and appeared

LAX RAT

in more than forty movies; he has organized and worked for a variety of social causes; and to this day, he is the only individual to be inducted in both the College Football Hall of Fame and the Lacrosse Hall of Fame. After his first year in the NFL, he was inducted into that hall of fame as well.

Jim Brown played for Syracuse University in four different sports, including lacrosse, though he is most famous as a football player.

LACROSSE

6
The Dangers of Performance-Enhancing Drugs

Understanding the Words

Inflammation *is the swelling and redness that is the body's response to injury or shock.*

To **stimulate** *means to encourage something to happen, to trigger a response.*

Infertility *is the inability to produce sperm or eggs; someone who is infertile cannot have biological children.*

An **electrolyte** *is a salt or mineral that conducts electrical impulses in the body; electrolytes are necessary for good health.*

If you have a **potassium deficiency,** *you lack enough potassium—one of the body's necessary electrolytes—to be healthy.*

A **hormone** *is a chemical in your body that helps control and regulate the activity of a body system (such as your reproductive system).*

Insomnia *is a condition where you are unable to fall asleep.*

Hypertension *is the medical term for having high blood pressure.*

A **hallucination** *is when a person sees something or someone that is not really there.*

LACROSSE

LAX RAT

For many professional players, the pressure to perform well is intense. Athletes face stress from everyone around them to constantly improve their skill, strength, and speed on the lacrosse field. Sometimes, an athlete turns to chemical enhancements to reach a level of competitive play of which he would not normally be capable. This is never legal, and is almost always dangerous, but nevertheless, some players feel compelled to use performance-enhancing drug.

What Are Drugs?

In general, a drug is anything that you place into your body that changes your body's chemistry in some way. Drugs can be useful or beneficial, such as the tablets you might take when you have a headache or antibiotics developed to fight diseases. Steroids are drugs useful for certain people with debilitating conditions that cause their muscles to waste away, and steroids can also be used to decrease inflammation. However, many drugs, including anabolic steroids, can have serious negative effects on your health.

Steroids

The most common performance enhancers are anabolic steroids. These chemicals are similar to testosterone, which is the male hormone naturally produced by the body to help stimulate muscle growth. That's why when a player takes anabolic steroids, he receives a boost to his speed and strength that is greater than what the body could normally produce on its own. Almost every organized sport considers this cheating.

Steroids can cause an unhealthy increase in cholesterol levels and an increase in blood pressure. This stresses the heart and leads to an increased risk of heart disease. Large doses of steroids can also lead to liver failure, and they have a negative effect on blood sugar levels, sometimes causing problems similar to diabetes. Steroids can also cause infertility.

If an adolescent (typically someone under the age of about seventeen) takes anabolic steroids, the risks are often much worse. Steroids stop bones from growing, which results in stunted growth. In addition, the risks to the liver and heart are much greater, since a young person's liver and heart are not fully matured and are more susceptible to the damage that steroids can cause. Furthermore, taking steroids puts you at a greater risk of psychological problems that generally begin with aggression but often lead to much more serious issues. Considering these health risks, as well as the fact that anabolic steroids are almost universally banned from organized sports, they should not be used, except by those who have legitimate medical conditions that require their use.

Steroids have legal uses, but they are also sold illegally. This bag of steroids was confiscated during a drug bust by the U.S. Drug Enforcement Agency.

LAX RAT

What Lacrosse Professionals Have to Say About Steroids

Ted Jenner, two-time Mann Cup champion and six-year veteran of the National Lacrosse League:

> **"There is no room for steroids in the 'little brother of war' . . . illegal substances of any kind can only hamper a lacrosse player's ability in a sport where it is all about hand-eye coordination, quickness, and stick skills. A clouded mind can only hamper a lacrosse player's ability to play at the top of his game."**
>
> **"Our players pride themselves on being the most natural of natural athletes. We work out, we train and**

Illicit Drugs

Sometimes, players use other drugs unrelated to boosting performance. There are severe penalties for using these drugs, and the drugs' side effects will usually decrease performance on the field. That's why professional lacrosse players don't usually use illegal drugs such as cocaine, LSD, and opiates.

LACROSSE

LAX RAT

we strive to be the best we can, but we also know that sacrificing skill for size doesn't benefit us in any way."

Michael Spinner, College of Notre Dame Athletic Director: "Lacrosse . . . [is] the combination of brains and brawn, and speed, and a craftiness that one does not necessarily need to succeed in other sports. When you think about it, being a 'great athlete' is only one facet of being a great lacrosse player. Having the innate ability to see a cutter coming off a pick and hitting him with the perfect feed right on his stick as a defender wails away at your gloves is a feat of athleticism. . . . And the most amazing thing about such a play is that all of the steroids in the world won't allow a lacrosse player to do it any better."

Diuretics

Diuretics are a class of drugs that increases urine production. Some athletes also believe that diuretics help them pass drug testing, since they dilute their urine. However, taking diuretics can upset the body's **electrolyte** balance and lead to dehydration. Taking diuretics such as acetazolamide (Diamox) can lead to muscle cramps, exhaustion, dizziness, **potassium deficiency**, a drop in blood pressure, and even death.

Androstenedione

Androstenedione is a **hormone** produced naturally by the adrenal glands, ovaries, and testes, which is then converted to testosterone and estadiol, the human sex hormones. Artificially produced androstenedione is a controlled substance that is illegal in competition in the United States, though it is still being sold.

Scientific evidence suggests that androstenodione doesn't promote muscle growth, and it has several serious risks. In men, side effects include acne, diminished sperm production, shrunken testicles, and enlargement of breasts. In women, the drug causes acne and masculinization, such as growth of facial hair. Androstenedione has also been shown to increase the chances of a heart attack and stroke because it causes the buildup of bad cholesterol.

Stimulants

Stimulants are a class of drugs that increase breathing rate, heart rate, and blood circulation. Athletes believe these drugs stimulate their central nervous system, allowing them to perform better. Stimulants such as caffeine, cold remedies, and street drugs (cocaine and methamphetamine) can promote alertness, suppress appetite, and increase aggressiveness. However, these drugs can also make an athlete have difficulty concentrating, as well as **insomnia**, nervousness, and irritability. Athletes can even become psychologically addicted. Other side effects include weight loss, tremors, heart rate abnormalities, **hypertension**, **hallucinations**, and heart attacks.

Over-the-Counter Drugs

Besides these dangerous and often illegal drugs, athletes also use painkillers and sedatives to enhance their performance. Painkillers allow athletes

to operate with a higher level of pain tolerance, while sedatives allow them to concentrate under stressful situations. However, these drugs can also decrease performance—and they can disqualify an athlete from competing if they are detected in his bloodstream.

The Consequences of Performance-Enhancing Drug Use

Lacrosse players, like all athletes, are often looking for a greater competitive edge to gain fame, acclaim, or an award or prize. However, there is no magical concoction that will automatically bring these rewards. Instead, these performance-enhancing drugs have many adverse side effects that could harm the body and its performance more than they help.

In late 2009, U.S. Lacrosse became an official member of the United States Anti-Doping Agency, or USADA. This group works with a number of national sports organizations to keep play fair for all athletes, and ensure a

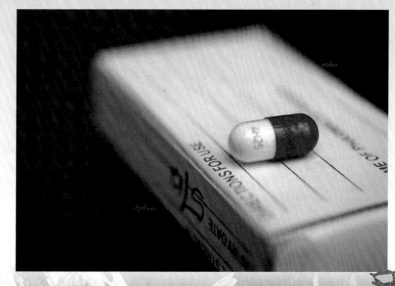

Taking something as ordinary—and legal— as Benadryl® can decrease your ability to perform well during a game.

safe environment. The USADA works with U.S. Lacrosse in drug testing, drug education, and teaching healthy lifestyles. In addition to drug testing, the USADA's mission is to educate coaches and athletes about substances that are sold as legal performance enhancers in nutrition stores and online.

The CEO of the USADA, Travis Tygart, explains that what's most alarming about this frightening trend is that

the average consumer of today is likely taking these products under the misconception that they are improving their health, when in fact they may be putting themselves in serious jeopardy. As a result, it's extremely important that you consult with your doctor, coach, or nutritionist before you begin taking any dietary supplements—without knowing all the facts, you could be endangering your body.

Some of the Best Lacrosse Players

You don't need performance-enhancing drugs to excel at lacrosse. The most well-known and accomplished lacrosse players are neither bulky nor take steroids or any other drugs of any kind.

Pat McCabe of the Long Island Lizards, for example, known as one of the best longsticks to ever play the sport, played lacrosse in college at Syracuse University, and thirteen years later, is still among the best defensemen in the world—but in spite of such a legendary reputation, McCabe doesn't exactly have the physical appearance of a world-class athlete: he is only 5'9" tall and is in no way considered the "strongest" or "fastest" in his sport. However, he has incredible knowledge of the game and excellent instincts, neither of which could be created or helped by steroids or any other drug.

Mark Millon, who played for the University of Massachusetts and now the Baltimore Bayhawks, is also a guy that is about average height. He too is 5'9" and definitely not what you would refer to as "jacked." In fact, if you saw Millon

LAX RAT

in street clothes, you might not even point him out as an athlete. But Millon is actually one of the leading attackmen in lacrosse today. He has great speed, vision, and great stick skills—and again, none of those qualities could be improved by performance-enhancing drugs.

So if the best players on the lacrosse field don't need performance-enhancing drugs—you don't either!

Further Reading

ASEP. *Coaching Youth Lacrosse*. Champaign, Ill.: Human Kinetics Publishers, 2003.

Gamble, Paul. *Strength and Conditioning for Team Sports: Sport-Specific Physical Preparation for High Performance*. New York: Routledge, 2010.

Perez-Mazzola, Vincent. *The Lacrosse Training Bible: The Complete Guide for Men and Women*. Long Island City, N.Y.: Hatherleigh Press, 2007.

Pietramala, David G. and Neil A. Grauer. *Lacrosse: Technique and Tradition, The Second Edition of the Bob Scott Classic*. Baltimore, Md.: The Johns Hopkins University Press, 2006.

Price, Robert G. *Ultimate Guide to Weight Training for Lacrosse*. New York: Sportsworkout.com, 2005.

Runk, Carl. *Carl Runk's Coaching Lacrosse: Strategies, Drills, & Plays from an NCAA Tournament Winning Coach's Playbook*. Columbus, Ohio: McGraw-Hill, 2009.

Find Out More on the Internet

Lax Links
www.laxlinks.com

Major League Lacrosse
www.majorleaguelacrosse.com

National Lacrosse League
www.nll.com

NCAA—Men's Lacrosse
www.ncaa.com/sports/m-lacros/ncaa-m-lacros-body.html

NCAA—Women's Lacrosse
www.ncaa.com/sports/w-lacros/ncaa-w-lacros-body.html

Sports Injury Info—Lacrosse Injuries
www.sports-injury-info.com/lacrosse-injuries.html

US Lacrosse
www.uslacrosse.org/Home.aspx

Women's Lacrosse
www.womenslacrosse.com/index_2.html

Disclaimer

The websites listed on this page were active at the time of publication. The publisher is not responsible for websites that have changed their address or discontinued operation since the date of publication. The publisher will review and update the websites upon each reprint.

Bibliography

Bureau of Labor Statistics. "Dieticians and Nutritionists," www.bls.gov/oco/ocos077.htm (10 March 2010).

e-Lacrosse. "The Roil Over Roids: Steroids, Newsweek, and the 'Lacrosse Image,'" www.e-lacrosse.com/2004/spin/36.html (17 March 2010).

Kidipede. "Centrifugal Force," www.historyforkids.org/scienceforkids/physics/machines/centrifugalforce.htm (8 March 2010).

Lacrosse Information. "Jim Brown Lacrosse," www.lacrosse-information.com/jim-brown-lacrosse.html (15 March 2010).

Mayo Clinic. "Concussion," www.mayoclinic.com/health/concussion/DS00320 (8 March 2010).

Medicine.net. "Definition of Contusion," www.medterms.com/script/main/art.asp?articlekey=2838 (10 March 2010).

Medicine.net. "Muscle Spasms," www.medicinenet.com/muscle_spasms/page2.htm (10 March 2010).

NLL Insider. "Steroids? We Don't Need No Stinking Steroids!" www.nllinsider.com/2009/02/17/steroids-we-dont-need-no-stinking-steroids/ (17 March 2010).

Orange Hoops. "Jim Brown," www.orangehoops.org/jbrown.htm (10 March 2010).

Rankin, Michael R. "Plyometrics," www.drexeldragons.com/documents/2008/6/9/plyometrics.pdf (8 March 2010).

TopTenz.net. "Top 10 Sports Figures Whose Careers are Tarnished by Steroids," www.toptenz.net/top-10-sports-figures-steroids.php (15 March 2010).

U.S. Lacrosse. "US Lacrosse Joins Anti-Doping Agency in New Initiative," www.uslacrosse.org/UtilityNav/AboutTheSport/SportsScienceandSafety/AntiDopingInitiative.aspx (15 March 2010).

Wisegeek. "What Are Ligaments?" www.wisegeek.com/what-are-ligaments.htm (8 March 2010).

Index

Picture Credits

Able, Glen: p. 46
Canada's Sports Hall of Fame: p. 12
Creative Commons: pp. 50, 66, 87
Eraxion, Dreamstime: p. 62
FotoDesign: p. 45
Green, Len; Dreamstime: p. 76
Lotus Head: pp. 41, 73
Monaghan, Timothy; Creative Commons: p. 79
Rozhenyuk, Alexander; Dreamstime: p. 75
Scholiers, G.A.: p. 70
Smithsonian Museum: p. 11
U.S. Drug Enforcement Agency: p. 82
U.S. Navy: p. 50
Vohsen, Kimberly: p. 42

To the best knowledge of the publisher, all images not specifically credited are in the public domain. If any image has been inadvertently uncredited, please notify Harding House Publishing Service, 220 Front Street, Vestal, New York 13850, so that credit can be given in future printings.

About the Author and the Consultants

Gabrielle Vanderhoof is a former competitive figure skater. She now works in publishing and public relations. This is her first time writing for Mason Crest.

Susan Saliba, Ph.D., is a senior associate athletic trainer and a clinical instructor at the University of Virginia in Charlottesville, Virginia. A certified athletic trainer and licensed physical therapist, Dr. Saliba provides sports medicine care, including prevention, treatment, and rehabilitation for the varsity athletes at the university. Dr. Saliba is a member of the national Athletic Trainers' Association Educational Executive Committee and its Clinical Education Committee.

Eric Small, M.D., a Harvard-trained sports medicine physician, is a nationally recognized expert in the field of sports injuries, nutritional supplements, and weight management programs. He is author of *Kids & Sports* (2002) and is Assistant Clinical professor of pediatrics, Orthopedics, and Rehabilitation Medicine at Mount Sinai School of Medicine in New York. He is also Director of the Sports Medicine Center for Young Athletes at Blythedale Children's Hospital in Valhalla, New York. Dr. Small has served on the American Academy of Pediatrics Committee on Sports Medicine, where he develops national policy regarding children's medical issues and sports.